# The Story of Flight

# COMMERCIAL AVIATION

# Crabtree Publishing Company
www.crabtreebooks.com

PMB 16A, 350 Fifth Avenue,
Suite 3308
New York, NY 10118

612 Welland Avenue
St. Catharines, Ontario
L2M 5V6

Published in 2003 by
**Crabtree Publishing Company**

**Coordinating editor:** Ellen Rodger
**Project editors:** Sean Charlebois, Carrie Gleason
**Production coordinator:** Rose Gowsell

Created and Produced by
**David West ⚇ Children's Books**

**Project Development, Design, and Concept**
David West Children's Books:
**Designer:** Rob Shone
**Editor:** James Pickering
**Illustrators:** James Field & Ross Watton (SGA), Gary
Slater & Steve Weston (Specs Art), Colin Howard
(Advocate), Alex Pang
**Picture Research:** Carlotta Cooper

06 05 04 03

10 9 8 7 6 5 4 3 2 1

Printed and bound in Dubai

Cataloging in Publication Data
Hansen, Ole Steen.
 Commercial aviation / by Ole Steen Hansen.
 p. cm. -- (The story of flight)
Includes index.
ISBN 0-7787-1205-2 (RLB) -- ISBN 0-7787-1221-4 (PB)
 1. Aeronautics, Commercial--History--Juvenile literature.
2. Airlines--History--Juvenile literature. [1. Aeronautics,
Commercial. 2. Airlines--History.] I. Title. II. Series.
 HE9774.H36 2003
 387.7'42--dc21
 2002156484
 LC

# The Story of Flight

# COMMERCIAL AVIATION

## Ole Steen Hansen

Crabtree Publishing Company
www.crabtreebooks.com

# CONTENTS

**FLYING IN STYLE**
Passengers flew in style on HP 42 airliners in the 1930s, but compared to modern jets they were noisy and bumpy in turbulence **at lower** altitudes.

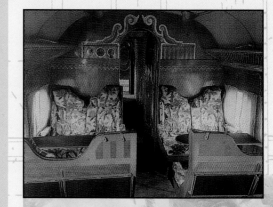

**A TRAGIC END TO THE AIRSHIPS**
The dramatic crash of the German airship Hindenburg in May 1937 marked the end of passenger flights in airships. Winged airplanes became the most important commercial aircraft.

# INTRODUCTION

Commercial flight took off immediately after World War I, even though passenger flights were cold, unsafe, and extremely expensive. As the years went by, airline passengers did not need to be wealthy or brave, as flying became cheaper and safer. In the 1950s, the first commercial jet aircraft appeared, and soon more people were crossing the Atlantic Ocean by air than by sea. Big jets eventually made flying the cheapest and safest way of traveling long distances.

BOEING 777
The Boeing 777 is a large, long distance jet with seating for up to 440 passengers. Engines have become so reliable that it is now safe for commercial aircraft with just two engines to cross the oceans.

# THE EARLY YEARS

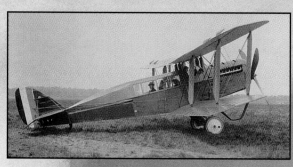

**AIR FORCE SURPLUS**
The world's first international scheduled air route was between London, England and Paris, France. It used single-engined DH 4A bombers from World War I. The converted planes carried two passengers in a small cabin behind the open cockpit where the pilot sat. The DH 16 (above) was built as an airliner in 1919. It carried four passengers in a covered rear cockpit.

**TAXI!**
Some people wanted to decide themselves when to take off and where to fly. Air taxis appeared as early as the first scheduled airlines. This Fokker C.II was used in Canada.

From the end of World War I in 1918, to the outbreak of World War II in 1939, great developments took place in commercial aviation. Modern air travelers would be shocked if they traveled back in time, and flew in these early airliners.

On long distance flights in airliners that were not air-conditioned, passengers had to think carefully about what clothes to wear. Over deserts, passengers were freezing in the morning and sweltering at noon. Vibration and noise from the big **piston engines** shook the cabins. On long routes, airliners often landed for the night, and crew and passengers slept in hotels.

In the years between the wars, airliners flew much lower than modern jets. With their big wings they bumped around in turbulence, and air sickness was common among passengers. There were good times too – days when passengers enjoyed good food, wonderful views from low level, and the knowledge they were lucky enough to be cruising over the continents on silver wings.

## The Way Ahead

The Douglas DC-3 aircraft first flew in 1935. It was the modern wonder of the 1930s with its retractable undercarriage or landing gear, and all-metal construction. The Douglas DC-3 was the **Allies'** most important cargo plane during World War II and the main plane of airlines all over the world after the war. Amazingly, some DC-3s are still being used today!

## DREAM MACHINES

Two important airliners between the wars were the British HP 42 (far left) and the German Junkers F-13 (right). Here, the airliners are flying out of Croydon, London, England's main airport after World War I. Passenger flights were more popular in Europe at the time than in North America. An Imperial Airways Armstrong Whitworth Argosy stands next to the HP 42. Coming in to land is a Farman Goliath.

# A GOLDEN AGE

## GOING TO EXTREMES
The Dornier Do X flying boat first flew in 1929, and it was then the world's biggest aircraft. It was never a big success, one problem being that its maximum altitude was only about 1,640 feet (500 m).

The time between the world wars was the golden age of the flying boat. Flying boats landed and docked in harbors near city centers all over the world. At the time, people thought flying boats would rule the airways over the oceans.

A major safety feature of flying boats was that they could land at sea if they had any technical trouble. To fly to South America from Europe, flying boats carrying mail had to land in the mid-Atlantic. Here, they were **hoisted** aboard a ship, refueled, and launched again from a **catapult**.

## PIGGYBACK PLANES
The Short Mayo Composite aircraft was built to increase the **range** of seaplanes, so they could fly across the Atlantic. The bigger flying boat lifted the smaller long-range airmail seaplane into the air. This way, the smaller seaplane did not waste fuel getting airborne. The small plane then continued on its own across the Atlantic.

By the summer of 1935, about four million letters had been flown across the Atlantic in flying boats. The big flying boats are best remembered as the jumbos of their day. They were both spacious and provided good service when carrying passengers. The British Short "C" Empire flying boat had a promenade deck where passengers enjoyed the view before having lunch or dinner, which was prepared in a well-stocked galley, or kitchen.

## CHINA CLIPPER

In 1935, the Martin M130 "China Clipper" established the first air route across the Pacific Ocean, from San Francisco to the Philippines. Here, a Clipper is flying past the Golden Gate Bridge in San Francisco, which was completed in 1937.

## Stewardesses

During the 1930s, airlines started to employ stewardesses. At first they were trained nurses, and worked in white uniforms. They cleaned the aircraft, carried baggage on board, and made sure the seats were fastened to the cabin floor. They also helped refuel the aircraft when it landed in remote places to let heavy weather pass. When airborne, handing out airsickness pills was just as important as serving food.

# POSTWAR AIR TRAVEL

The first jet airliners were flown in the 1950s. Most airline flights up until that time were made in propeller-driven, piston-engined aircraft. The DC-3 was the main aircraft of the air routes, but new aircraft were being developed too.

## STRATOCRUISER

Luxurious Boeing Stratocruiser airliners were built between 1947 and 1950. They were equipped with a lounge and sleeping bunks for passengers. The Stratocruiser was developed from the World War II B-29 bomber.

## OVER THE NORTH POLE

Big, piston-engined aircraft such as the DC-6 and DC-7 could fly over the North Pole in the 1950s. The problem was that compasses did not work over the Pole. The navigator had to rely on the position of the stars, until new navigational systems were developed. After that, airlines started flying from Northern Europe to North America and Japan over the North Pole. The distance from Northern Europe to the west and east coasts of North America is the same if the aircraft is flown over the North Pole and therefore this route saves fuel. It also cut down on flying time to Japan from Europe.

Japan

North America

North Pole

Northern Europe

The United States led the way in developing new airliners after World War II. During the war, the four-engined DC-4 and the Lockheed Constellation had been produced as military transport planes. These aircraft were quickly turned into airliners. They were far bigger than the airliners flown before the war, and they needed longer runways. Runways had been built for bombers all over the world during the war. Now they were used for the new generation of airliners. Airliners in the postwar years provided good service to the lucky people who were wealthy enough to fly in them. The United States was the world's largest producer of airliners. In 1946, over 12 million people flew on American domestic flights – two thirds of all the airline passengers worldwide.

## CONNIE – QUEEN OF THE AIRWAYS

The Lockheed Constellation, often referred to as "Connie," was one of the most popular airliners after World War II. Some Connies were still flying passengers in the 1960s. Many people consider Connie one of the most beautiful airliners ever built.

## DC-7

Scandinavian Airlines pioneered flights over the Arctic. In 1957, a DC-7 flew from Copenhagen, Denmark, to Tokyo, Japan, over the North Pole. Today, airliners rarely use the North Pole route, because aircraft can now fly longer without refueling.

# JET TRAVEL

## CARAVELLE
The French Caravelle first flew in 1955. It was the world's first short- and medium-range jet airliner. It was also the first airliner to have its engines mounted at the tail.

J et planes were a huge improvement over earlier airliners. Not only were jet airliners faster, but they produced less noise from the engines. Jets only vibrated a little, and they were twice as fast as propeller-driven planes.

## DH 106 COMET
The DH 106 Comet had its first flight in 1949. It entered airline service in 1952, when the world's first jet passengers checked in for a flight from London, England to Johannesburg, South Africa.

Air pressure at ground level

Air pressure at high altitude

## PRESSURIZED CABINS
A submarine is built to survive heavy pressure from the outside. A jet airliner is designed to withstand heavy pressure from the inside when flying at high altitude. At high altitude, the air pressure outside the plane is much lower than at ground level. A pressurized cabin means that passengers do not need special clothing and oxygen masks.

Jets also flew above most of the turbulent weather below. Jet airliners were a major step forward in making air travel more comfortable, but safety was a concern. Three de Havilland Comet jets ruptured in mid-air after only a year of service. The investigations into the crashes showed that the airframe, or body of the plane, weakened when it pressurized and depressurized. It was discovered that jet airliners needed to be built stronger than the Comets. The American airline company Boeing learned from the mistakes in the construction of the Comet, and began to build their own jet airliners, which were much safer.

**Boeing 707**
The Boeing 707 jet was built in 1957, and it was the world's first intercontinental jet airliner. The aircraft was developed using experience from bomber aircraft such as the Boeing B-47 and B-52. The idea of swept-back wings, combined with **pylon**-mounted engines, was inspired by German research during World War II. Many Boeing 707s still fly today.

## LOCKHEED 14

**Country**: USA
**Length**: 43 ft 10 in
(13.5 m)
**Wingspan**: 65 ft (20 m)
**Cruising Speed**: 240 mph
(386 km/h)
**Range**: 1,000 miles (1,600 km)
**Capacity**: 12
**Engines**: 2 radial
piston engines

## PISTON ENGINE

Piston engines were used in older airliners such as the Ju 52, DC-6, and Lockheed 14. The constant moving up and down of parts created a lot of vibration.

## TURBOPROP

This is a turbine jet engine that uses its energy to turn a propeller. On a turboprop aircraft you can hear the sound of the propeller mixed with the whine of the jet engine.

## FOKKER F27 FRIENDSHIP MK200

**Country**: Netherlands
**Length**: 77 ft 3 in (23.6 m)
**Wingspan**: 95 ft 2 in (29 m)
**Cruising Speed**: 302 mph (486 km/h)
**Range**: 1,200 miles (1,930 km)
**Capacity**: 48
**Engines**: 2 turboprops

## ENGINE CONFIGURATIONS

Some engines are mounted in the wings. More commonly, the engines are under the wings in pylons, as on the Boeing 747. Mounting engines at the tail gives better air flow over the wings and creates less noise in the cabin.

## GATES LEARJET MODEL 24

**Country**: USA
**Length**: 43 ft 3 in (13.2 m)
**Wingspan**: 35 ft 7 in (10.8 m)
**Cruising Speed**: 481 mph (770 km/h)
**Range**: 2,700 miles (4,345 km)
**Capacity**: 6
**Engines**: 2 turbojets

# POWER PLANTS

**E**arly commercial aircraft had piston engines that worked similarly to car engines. Most airliners today have turbojets, turbofans, or turboprops, which are turbine, or jet, engines. They are very reliable and free from vibration.

## ENGINE MAINTENANCE
Reliable modern turbine engines are maintained using strict standards and procedures. Aircraft are often serviced at night and the ground crew work in shifts.

## TURBOFAN
In a turbofan engine, a big fan at the front pushes air around the engine. The fast-moving, noisy air from the exhaust is mixed with the slower air from the fan, resulting in a quieter engine.

## LOCKHEED L-1011 TRISTAR 1
**Country**: USA
**Length**: 162 ft 6 in (50 m)
**Wingspan**: 162 ft 6 in (50 m)
**Cruising Speed**: 578 mph (925 km/h)
**Range**: 2,900 miles (4,670 km)
**Capacity**: 345
**Engines**: 3 turbofans

CF-TNB

AIR CANADA

## TURBOJET
In a turbojet engine, air is sucked in and compressed. In the combustion chamber, fuel is burned which causes the air to expand. The hot air forces its way out at the rear of the engine, turning a turbine on a shaft, which is connected to the compressor at the front, sucking in more air.

### Flight Engineer
In the cockpit of the Concorde, the flight engineer monitors the engine instruments, while two pilots fly the plane. Earlier jets, such as the Boeing 707, also had three crew members in the cockpit. On newer jets, computers have taken over the job of the flight engineer.

# BOEING 747–PEOPLE CARRIER

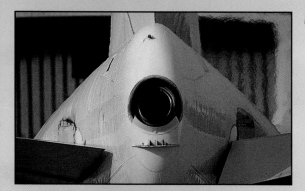

**GROUND POWER**
The jumbo jet has a 1,100 horsepower APU (Auxiliary Power Unit) in the tail that provides power when the big engines are shut down on the ground.

The 747 jet airliner was a big gamble for the Boeing company. It was so expensive to develop that a failure would have ruined the company. Would airlines buy an aircraft that was so much bigger than existing jets? Would there be enough passengers wanting to fly and buy the tickets?

The gamble paid off. More than 1,000 Boeing 747s have been built. The Jumbos were expensive to buy and fly, but they carried so many passengers that the price per seat dropped. More people could afford to fly, and they did when the price was right. The big jets made travel between the continents easier for millions of people around the world.

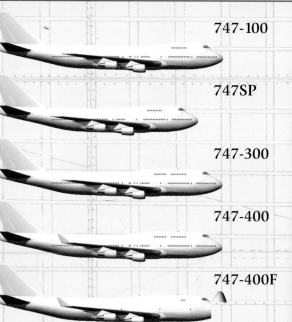

747-100

747SP

747-300

747-400

747-400F

**747 FAMILY**
The Jumbo has been produced in different versions. The first was the 747-100 "Classic." The latest is the 747-400, which has an extended upper deck, greater wingspan and almost twice the range. The 400F is a transport version. The 747SP was an early long-range version, but the 747-400 flies longer.

### At The Controls

The Boeing 747-400 has 600 fewer switches and instruments in the cockpit than earlier versions, because so much is displayed on computer screens. The pilots still have to handle or monitor 365 switches and instruments. The front window of the cockpit is 2 inches (5 cm) thick. It will not break if it hits a large bird at high speed.

The large 747s have carried so many passengers that the number equals 25 percent of the world's population. The Boeing 747 is one of the greatest success stories in the history of aviation. It takes about six million parts to build a 747. The parts come from as far away as Japan, Australia, Korea, and Britain to the assembly line in the United States.

### UP AND AWAY

Singapore Airlines is a major Asian airline that uses 39 Boeing 747-400s on its routes from the tiny island state of Singapore to other places in Asia, the United States, Australia, and Europe.

## IN THE WILDERNESS

In northern and western Canada and Alaska, float planes are used to serve small communities near lakes and rivers. Companies also fly tourists out to camp or fish in the wilderness where no other vehicles can take them. Passengers can even go on a "float plane safari."

## STOL

Helicopters carry people and cargo everywhere, but they are slow, expensive, and have limited range. Winged aircraft do it more quickly and cheaply, and STOL aircraft (Short Take-Off and Landing) only need short runways. The de Havilland Canada DHC-7 is a large four-engined STOL aircraft that flies up to 50 passengers to landing strips where no other aircraft of its size can land.

# OUT OF THE WAY PLACES

In many places around the world small aircraft serve islands and remote communities. They make it possible for the people there to stay in contact with the rest of the world.

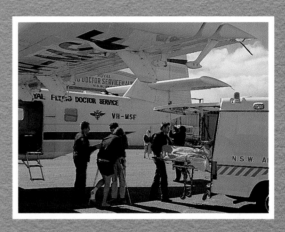

**JOEY**

On an island called Aurigny in the British Isles, a plane called "Joey" is a character in a series of children's books. Joey is based on a real aircraft, Trislander, but in the books it almost has a mind of its own.

Float planes have floats instead of wheels for landing gear, so they can land or take-off from water. Float planes are commonly used in Alaska, northern Canada, and all along the west coast of North America. Planes called Amphibians have both floats and retractable landing gear with wheels, so they can land on water or on land. On small islands all over the world, people in remote communities depend upon these aircraft to bring them supplies. The pilots who fly in these places need to be especially skilled.

**Flying Doctor**

In Australia, the Royal Flying Doctor Service was founded in 1928 to provide remote communities with a fast emergency health service. Today, it operates a fleet of modern ambulance aircraft from 20 bases around the country and is ready to help 365 days a year.

Often, there is no radar on the ground to guide pilots on their way. The weather can change quickly and without warning. Storms can toss their small airplanes around in narrow mountain passes.

# SUPERSONIC LUXURY

The Concorde is the world's only supersonic airliner. It was not difficult building an aircraft that flew at Mach 2, or twice the speed of sound. Military aircraft already did that, but only for a few minutes at a time.

## FLIGHT DECK

Concorde was first flown in 1969, and it still looks like a new aircraft. It was built at a time when cockpits had many dials and switches and no computer screens.

BRITISH AIRWAYS

## FUEL TRANSFER

When Concorde accelerates to supersonic speed, the nose of the aircraft becomes very heavy. The pilot could lift the nose with a touch of the **elevator** but this would increase **drag** on the aircraft and burn up fuel too fast. When Concorde reaches supersonic speed, fuel is transferred to tanks in the rear of the aircraft. This balances the aircraft so it will not fall nose-first from the sky.

SUBSONIC

Rear tank

SUPERSONIC

Forward tanks

To build an airliner that could fly for over three hours at Mach 2 and still carry passengers to pay for the flight was more difficult. Other challenges were caused by the heating of the aircraft.

When flying at Mach 2, **air resistance** becomes so great that the airframe is heated in parts to more than 212°F (100°C). This causes the outside of the airframe to expand, as metals do when they are heated. At the same time, temperature inside the aircraft had to be comfortable for passengers. To build the Concorde meant building an aircraft that expanded in places, but not in others.

**A RARE BIRD**

Only 14 Concordes were ever put into service. They are very expensive to fly in and have largely remained something for the rich and famous. Sometimes Concordes have done special charters for people who wanted to have a short flight at Mach 2. In 1999, Concorde flights were arranged for people to see the solar eclipse at **supersonic speed**.

### Concordski

The Soviet Tupolev Tu-144 supersonic airliner was designed as a competitor to the British-French Concorde. Its close resemblance to the Concorde resulted in it being nicknamed "Concordski." The Tu-144 actually flew a few months earlier than Concorde, but it was never a success and was used only briefly on airmail flights. After some of the jets crashed, they were all withdrawn from service. Concorde has remained the only supersonic airliner in the history of aviation.

## VICKERS VISCOUNT 810
**Country**: Britain
**Length**: 85 ft 8 in (26.1 m)
**Wingspan**: 93 ft 8 in (28.5 m)
**Cruising Speed**: 350 mph (563 km/h)
**Range**: 1,300 miles (2,090 km)
**Capacity**: 71

## HAWKER SIDDELEY HS. 121 TRIDENT
**Country**: Britain
**Length**: 114 ft 9 in (35 m)
**Wingspan**: 98 ft (29.9 m)
**Cruising Speed**: 596 mph (960 km/h)
**Range**: 2,600 miles (4,180 km)
**Capacity**: 149

## BOEING 737-200
**Country**: USA
**Length**: 100 ft (30.5 m)
**Wingspan**: 93 ft (28.3 m)
**Cruising Speed**: 576 mph (927 km/h)
**Range**: 2,400 miles (3,860 km )
**Capacity**: 130

## McDONNELL DOUGLAS DC-9 SRS 50
**Country**: USA
**Length**: 119 ft (36.4 m)
**Wingspan**: 93 ft 5 in (28.5 m)
**Cruising Speed**: 572 mph (918 km/h)
**Range**: 1,600 miles (2,575 km)
**Capacity**: 122–139

## Sir Freddie Laker
As a young man, Frederick Alfred Laker worked with Short Brothers, who built the big Empire flying boats. He eventually set up a number of his own airlines. Laker is remembered for his Skytrain service, which opened up the Atlantic airspace for the general public because of its low-cost flights. Unfortunately, Sir Freddie's business failed, but he paved the way for the low-cost airlines of today.

## AIRBUS A320
**Country**: Spain, France, Britain, Germany
**Length**: 123 ft 2 in (37.8 m)
**Wingspan**: 111 ft 10 in (34.5 m)
**Cruising Speed**: 560 mph (986 km/h)
**Range**: 3,340 miles (5,344 km)
**Capacity**: 180

# AIRLINES

Airlines are companies that make money by flying passengers and cargo. The colors on the aircraft, the service on board, how well they keep to the promised schedule, and the price of the ticket are ways of attracting customers.

Airlines offer a fast and safe way of transporting people. They all do this, and they fly much the same types of planes. Why do passengers choose one instead of the other? In recent years there has been a lot of emphasis on the price. Economy class airfares were introduced in 1952, but were still too expensive for most people. In the 1970s, a man from Britain, Sir Freddie Laker, used big jets to introduce low-cost flying across the Atlantic. Today, low-cost carriers are operating jets over shorter distances, too. These airlines are growing more quickly than any others. Flying is often the cheapest way to travel from one place to another, though in-flight drinks and refreshments are extra.

**BIG RESPRAY JOB**
The markings on an aircraft tell you what airline it belongs to. Airlines take a lot of care to ensure that the paint job on their aircraft gives them a modern and attractive image. Airlines usually change their aircraft colors every few years.

Boeing 747 business class

Boeing 747 economy class

**COMFY SEATS?**
In economy class, the Boeing 747 has more seats than in business class. The business class seats are wider, more comfortable, and spaced wider apart. The prices for business class tickets are also higher. People decide whether they want more comfortable seats or lower prices. Only one thing is certain – flying with empty seats is awfully expensive for the airlines!

Scandinavian Airlines

www.MyTravel.com  G-CGEZ  MY TRAVEL

# AIRPORT

**A**irports are the crossroads of the world. Sitting in the departure lounge of a big international airport, you will see people from all over the world. Just a day later, big jets will have flown them to every corner of the globe.

Airports handle enormous numbers of passengers. Over 100 million people pass through London, England airports annually – more than 270,000 each day! Chicago and Atlanta airports handle more than 900,000 flights a year – around 2,500 aircraft flights a day.

## INTO THE AIRCRAFT

Modern terminals have gangways that allow passengers to walk directly into their aircraft. They may not even see the aircraft before they are inside!

## FIRE TRUCK

Fire trucks are always ready to go into action at short notice, but are rarely needed.

## Air Traffic Control

Passengers rarely see other aircraft in the sky – but they are there, especially around the major airports. Aircraft are closely followed by radar and air traffic controllers. The controllers give pilots directions so that aircraft are kept at safe distances from each other.

## FUEL TANKER

Some aircraft are refueled from tankers, while pipelines in the ground are used to refuel others. A Boeing 747 might burn over 14 tons (13 tonnes) of fuel every hour. For a twelve-hour flight, a large amount of fuel is needed!

24

Airports need to be well organized, so people can easily get through customs and onto their planes. The aircraft has to be serviced quickly to spend as little time as possible on the ground. At the airport there are many different vehicles built for specific tasks.

## PLANE TUG

It is cheaper and quicker to move a big jet around an airport with a tug, instead of starting the engines of the aircraft.

## MOBILE STAIRWAY

Mobile stairs are used when aircraft park far away from the terminal gangways.

## SUPPLY VEHICLE

Food, drinks, and everything else needed to give the passengers a pleasant journey are brought to the aircraft in specialized supply vehicles.

## BAGGAGE TRAIN

Passengers' baggage is brought to and from the aircraft in small carriages.

1 Main runway
2 Airport lounge
3 Control tower
4 Railway station
5 Hangars
6 Customs
7 Service vehicle garage
8 Access road
9 Parking lot

## AIRPORT DESIGN

Big airports have two runways – one for landing and the other for take-off. That way, more flights can be handled. Passengers need to be able to get easily to and from the airport. Rail service and car-rental facilities are the most common ways.

# TODAY'S AIRLINERS

**SAAB 340**
Smaller airliners are still produced in a number of countries. The Swedish company Saab has had success with their 340 regional airliner. It seats up to 35 passengers and is used on shorter routes.

A t one time, the United States, Britain, France, Germany, and other countries all had their own companies producing airliners. Today, the development of high-tech aircraft has become so expensive that there are just two big jet companies in the world.

In the United States, Boeing is the only company that makes large jets. In Europe, companies from Britain, France, Germany, and Spain have formed Airbus. Only by working together have these European countries been able to compete with Boeing. Many countries around the world have bought American-made Boeing jets. Airbus has introduced a number of new aircraft to compete with Boeing.

**Flight Simulators**
Pilots are trained to handle all kinds of emergencies in flight simulators. On the inside, simulators look and feel like real cockpits. They move to give the feeling of an aircraft in flight. Pilots safely train for situations that would be unsafe to train for in a real aircraft.

The first Airbus, the A300 from 1972, had a better blind landing system than other airlines at the time, allowing it to land in poor **visibility**. The Airbus 340-500 is the world's longest range airliner, able to fly over 9,950 miles (16,000 km) non-stop, or more than a third of the way around the globe.

## PLANE CARRIER
The larger parts, such as the wings, are flown to assembly lines in freighter aircraft.

## FLY-BY-WIRE
The small twin-engined A320 airliner was the first to have "fly-by-wire" controls. From the sidestick in the cockpit, the pilot's instructions are sent to a computer. The computer then makes sure the controls are moved correctly. Fly-by-wire has several advantages, one being that the pilot cannot accidentally stall the aircraft. The computer will not let him or her do it!

## MULTINATIONAL
Airbus has 16 building sites in France, Germany, Great Britain, and Spain for their jets. In addition, 1,500 companies in over 30 countries supply parts to build the aircraft.

# TOMORROW'S AIRLINERS

**AIRBUS A380**

Originally called the A3XX-100, the A380 is supposed to make its first flight in 2004 and enter service in 2006. It will be the first modern airliner with twin decks along the length of the aircraft. Thanks to its sophisticated computer system, it will handle like a smaller airplane. Therefore, current Airbus pilots will find it easy to adapt to the A380.

## In-Flight Entertainment

As exciting as flying is, long non-stop flights during dark nights and high above the clouds can be boring. Flying times of 14 hours or more will become increasingly common as aircraft increase their range. Many airlines now offer a personal in-flight entertainment system in every seat. You can watch movies or play computer games.

**W**ithin the last 70 years, airliners have progressed from small and unsafe biplanes to jets flying passengers in great comfort high in the sky. What will the future hold for commercial flight? Will speed or the price of a ticket be the most important issue?

Low-cost airlines have had great success in recent years. The new Airbus A380 will make it even cheaper to fly. Speed is another reason why people choose to fly, rather than travel by train or ship. In the future, passengers will probably have to make the choice between price and speed. Even though the Concorde has never been widely used, there are still plans to build even faster aircraft. American researchers plan to fly the X-43 series of experimental aircraft at seven or more times the speed of sound. This will provide the knowledge and technology to fly passengers around the world at the edge of space, and at several times the speed of sound. Ticket prices will be very high, and only time will tell if there are enough passengers to fill the planes.

## X-43B

The X-43B is an unmanned research vehicle, able to fly at least seven times the speed of sound before gliding down to land on a runway.

## RAMJET

The engines for the X-43B will work similarly to an ordinary jet engine at supersonic speeds. For the dash up to maximum speed, the engine works like a ramjet, with air being pushed through and heated by the burning fuel. The Ramjet part is necessary for high speed flight, while the "old" jet engine is needed at low speed.

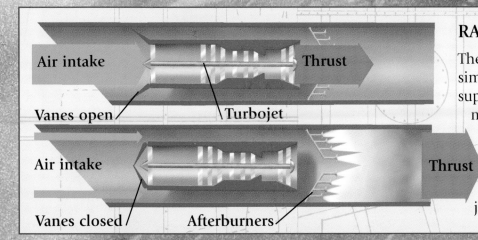

Air intake

Thrust

Vanes open

Turbojet

Air intake

Thrust

Vanes closed

Afterburners

# SPOTTERS' GUIDE

**R**eliable and powerful modern engines have made it possible to build bigger and better airliners. Each of the engines on the Constellation was as powerful as the China Clipper's four engines combined. Each engine on the Boeing 747 has more power than all four engines on the Constellation!

**JUNKERS F-13**
Country: Germany
Length: 31 ft 2 in (9.6 m)
Wingspan: 48 ft 2 in (14.8 m)
Cruising Speed: 87 mph (140 km/h)
Range: 875 miles (1,400 km)
Capacity: 4
First Flight: 1919

**DOUGLAS DC-3**
Country: USA
Length: 64 ft 6 in (19.7 m)
Wingspan: 95 ft (29 m)
Cruising Speed: 194 mph (312 km/h)
Range: 2,125 miles (3,420 km)
Capacity: 24
First Flight: 1935

**HANDLEY PAGE HP 42W**
Country: Britain
Length: 92 ft 2 in (28.1 m)
Wingspan: 130 ft (39.6 m)
Cruising Speed: 125 mph (204 km/h)
Range: 500 miles (805 km)
Capacity: 38
First Flight: 1930

**MARTIN MODEL 130 CHINA CLIPPER**
Country: USA
Length: 90 ft 10 in (27.7 m)
Wingspan: 130 ft (39.6 m)
Cruising Speed: 157 mph (252 km/h)
Range: 3,200 miles (5,150 km)
Capacity: 48
First Flight: 1935

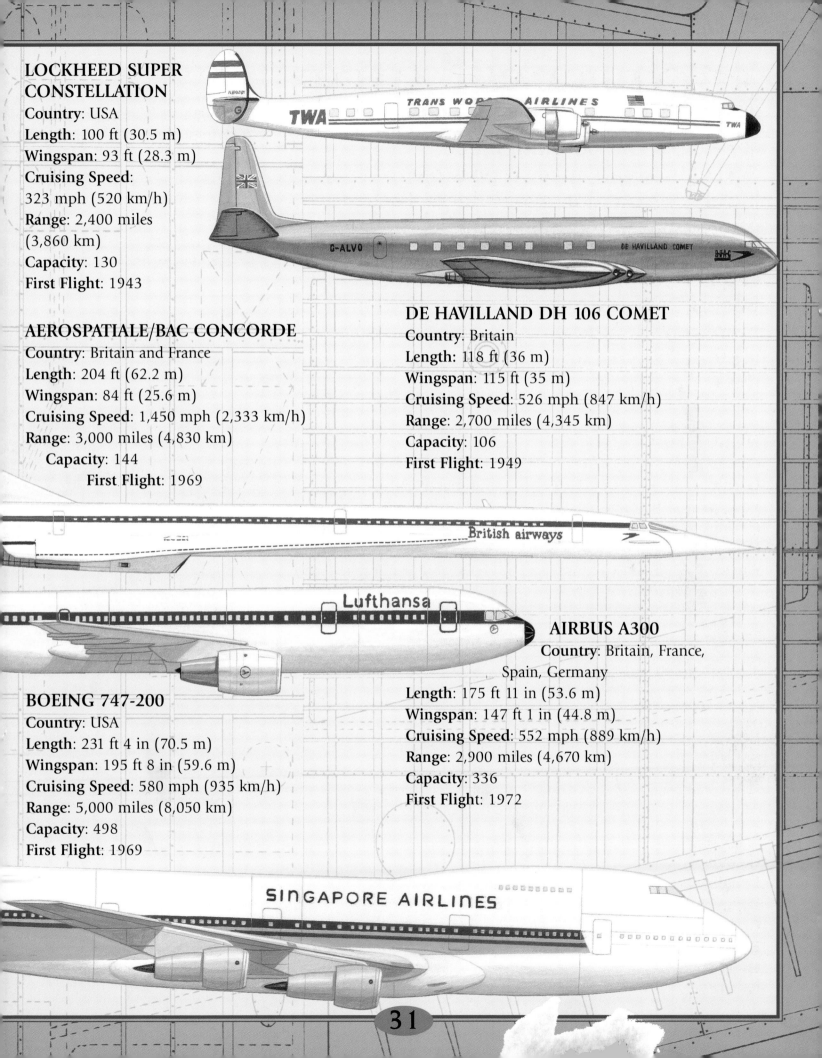

## LOCKHEED SUPER CONSTELLATION
**Country**: USA
**Length**: 100 ft (30.5 m)
**Wingspan**: 93 ft (28.3 m)
**Cruising Speed**: 323 mph (520 km/h)
**Range**: 2,400 miles (3,860 km)
**Capacity**: 130
**First Flight**: 1943

## DE HAVILLAND DH 106 COMET
**Country**: Britain
**Length**: 118 ft (36 m)
**Wingspan**: 115 ft (35 m)
**Cruising Speed**: 526 mph (847 km/h)
**Range**: 2,700 miles (4,345 km)
**Capacity**: 106
**First Flight**: 1949

## AEROSPATIALE/BAC CONCORDE
**Country**: Britain and France
**Length**: 204 ft (62.2 m)
**Wingspan**: 84 ft (25.6 m)
**Cruising Speed**: 1,450 mph (2,333 km/h)
**Range**: 3,000 miles (4,830 km)
**Capacity**: 144
**First Flight**: 1969

## AIRBUS A300
**Country**: Britain, France, Spain, Germany
**Length**: 175 ft 11 in (53.6 m)
**Wingspan**: 147 ft 1 in (44.8 m)
**Cruising Speed**: 552 mph (889 km/h)
**Range**: 2,900 miles (4,670 km)
**Capacity**: 336
**First Flight**: 1972

## BOEING 747-200
**Country**: USA
**Length**: 231 ft 4 in (70.5 m)
**Wingspan**: 195 ft 8 in (59.6 m)
**Cruising Speed**: 580 mph (935 km/h)
**Range**: 5,000 miles (8,050 km)
**Capacity**: 498
**First Flight**: 1969

# INDEX

# GLOSSARY

**AIR RESISTANCE** The pull of air on an object as it moves.

**AIRSHIP** An aircraft filled with a lighter than air gas and is self-propelled.

**ALLIES** The nations that fought together against the Axis powers (Germany, Italy, and Japan) in WWII, including Britain, France, the United States, and the Soviet Union.

**ALTITUDE** A height measured from sea level, or the Earth's surface.

**CATAPULT** A mechanical device for launching an aircraft from a ship.

**CHARTERS** Aircraft hired for a specific purpose.

**COMPRESSED** Packed tightly together in a small space.

**DEPARTURE** The place from which passengers board the aircraft.

**DRAG** The force that pulls back on an aircraft.

**ELEVATOR** The moveable part of a tail plane which makes the airplane climb or dive.

**HOIST** To raise up using a system of ropes and pulleys.

**JET** An aircraft with a engine, which causes forward motion by forcing hot gases from a rear opening.

**PISTON ENGINE** A circular disk that moves back and forth in a cylinder. In engines, pistons are moved by igniting fuel and air.

**PYLON** A structure on the wing of an aircraft that supports an engine.

**RANGE** The distance an aircraft is capable of flying with the fuel it has.

**SHAFT** A long narrow part supporting or driving another part.

**SOLAR ECLIPSE** An event in which the Sun's rays are prevented from reaching Earth because the Moon is passing between them.

**TURBULENCE** Stormy air caused by an air current moving against the flow of the main current.

**VISIBILITY** The amount that can be seen.